Digital Transformation

The Significant 7 Imperatives for Delivering Successful Change in Complex IT Projects

By Martin Sharp & Edward Johns

Digital Transformation

Published by
10-10-10 Publishing
Markham, Ontario
CANADA

First Published in 2016

Copyright © 2016 Martin Sharp & Edward Johns
York, England, United Kingdom
www.thedigitaltransformationbook.com

For information about special discounts for bulk purchases, please contact 10-10-10 Publishing at 1-888-504-6257

Printed in the United States of America

ISBN-13: 978-1537785035
ISBN-10: 1537785036

Contents

DEDICATION   v

TESTIMONIALS   vii

ACKNOWLEDGEMENTS   ix

FOREWORD   xi

INTRODUCTION   1

THE CHANGE IMPERATIVE FOR IT   9

PRESSING BUSINESS & IT CHALLENGES   19

A FLEXIBLE FOUNDATION   31

STRUCTURED APPROACH   47

DELIVERING SUCCESS   61

DEMONSTRABLE BREADTH OF VALUE   71

DELIVERING REAL BENEFITS   81

THE SIGNIFICANT 7 IMPERATIVES FOR ALL IT PROJECTS   93

ABOUT THE AUTHORS   105

DEDICATION

This book is dedicated to all the consultants, architects, managers, engineers, developers and clients out there that we have worked with over the years. Their interactions, brilliance, and foibles served as our arena for learning, and ground zero for our trying new ideas.

It is with them that we have grown in our understanding and success. And it is with them that our futures will be full of more learning opportunities.

No book dedication would be complete without a homage being paid to our families who have stood by us in the good and bad times, tantrums and triumphs, over the years that it has taken us to get here.

Thank you.

TESTIMONIALS

Martin designed the IT Architecture for Spire Healthcare, a £1.5Bn private hospital provider. Our infrastructure was reliable, performant, scalable, and cost effective – a great result.

Martin, himself, is very personable, expert and reliable. He is a pleasure to do business with.

Marc O'Brien – Chief Information Officer – Spire Healthcare

Ed has vision, consummate planning and management skills, and an eye for the details. He is open and engaging, but, most importantly, he makes decisions and follows them through.

I thoroughly enjoyed working with Ed and can recommend him without any hesitation.

Simon Shearston –Chief Technologist - Microsoft

ACKNOWLEDGMENTS

We would like to thank all those people in our lives who have made our lives possible, going back to antiquity, as, without you, we would not have gained the experience that we needed in order to be able to write this book. We would like to specifically mention:

- Sarah Sharp, for proofreading, editing, and generally supporting Martin throughout the process.
- Rob Bamforth, Industry Analyst, without whom the 7 imperatives may have remained unnamed.
- Dom Ioanna, Designer and Developer, who helped bring the vision to life.
- Naval Kumar & Vishal Morjaria, Personal Book Architects, whose advice, guidance, and constant badgering helped get this book over the line.
- Lisa Browning, Editor, as the editor that took the draft manuscript and made it shine.
- Sufyan, Designer, who finalised and stylised all the diagrams.
- Ilian Georgiev, Designer, for taking the ideas from the book and designing the cover.
- David Feldman, Copy Writer, for creating the wording for the website.

- Laurence Yunghova, Copy Writer, assisting with wording and positioning.
- Shane Colombo and Steven Sperling, Entrepreneurs, for all the opportunities you have gotten us involved in, good and incredible.
- Andrew Mason, Serial Entrepreneur, who gave a kick at the right time to start the adventure.
- Dan Donnelly, Entrepreneur and good friend, for all the support over the years.
- Ian Kennedy, VP Operations, the man who believed in some of the riskier ideas, and supported doing them anyway.
- John Oddy, finance guru, business guru, friend and mentor. Wouldn't have gotten this far without him.
- Mark Overend, accountant and tax expert, keeping the business running.
- Asad Ali, legal expert and business advisor keeping us safe.
- Sean Gilks, financial advice.
- Stephen Varney, photographer for the more professional photographs.

FOREWORD

On a daily basis, when I am getting a coffee in an airport, or going from one meeting to another, the number one question that people ask me about life is how to accomplish a goal pertaining to a particular project. The answer is that it all comes down to goal setting, execution, and transformation. It is a second nature process to me. It would be something that I could map out in my head before they finish their question. It comes down to a simple transformation.

In the Information Technology field, this answer doesn't change at all. The secret to the answer is pretty simple. It is actually a quality that most Information Technology professionals have in them that is self-taught. I say self-taught because, in Information Technology, anyone who is in this field sits with a computer for long hours.

It is a bond that only they have with their brain in the form of a transformation. It triggers when they are working on a small to complex project. It is a skill that requires them to focus in order to make themselves see a problem, immediately know the root cause, and fix it on the fly, within split seconds. This also has to be related to a machine, the computer, that can do millions of small processes within an instant.

It is called programming, which is a fascinating process to me, but, to them, it is second nature. I could not do this, but they can. Some call it *the zone*. That laser-like problem, solution, resolution response, is a digital transformation. It is a battle, but, to one in this field, it comes second nature. It is a fascinating thing. I could never win that battle, but they do. I find it amazing.

What does it take to get everyone on board with the same thing? A goal – a common goal? It takes a smaller system. Another transformation. This one requires seven key skills in order to get everyone to make an imperative change in order for them to execute the vision. There are 7 imperatives that are critical to the whole project. Without them, you and your team cannot get into the individual zones that it will take to finalize execution. If this was an individual project, done by yourself, or anyone else on the team, the project would be no problem. The approach to getting into the minds of professionals within Information Technology, requires transformation. In order to deliver, the final delivery is key. It is the whole reason that you have picked up this book. This is why you have purchased this book. You will learn the keys to taking one transformation and scaling it.

Raymond Aaron
New York Times Top Ten Best Selling Author and Business Leader

.

INTRODUCTION

It is important to start at the beginning, yet, at the same time, you need to start with the end in mind. If you don't start with the end in mind, then you really don't have an idea of where you are going to go, or what you are going to do.

Those of us who have been lucky enough to run our own business, or manage a business, will realise that a company is like any person, in that it has its own identity and personality. Just like people, it has its own goal drivers and objectives that it is setting out to achieve for itself. These can be set out in the company mission statement, or vision statement, of which each area of the organisation then uses in another way to help themselves understand what the business is trying to do.

Anybody who has taken the time to look at really good businesses, will have noticed that these businesses have a great clarity of thinking that is well articulated, backed by a fantastic team of people who are helping to deliver the mission of vision and absolute alignment between the activities of the people working inside the business, and the objectives of the business.

These traits are how they're going to grow the company and fulfil its needs. So, with this in mind, why is it that so many projects (specifically IT projects), miss these simple steps? For this book, we are setting out some simple goals with the aim to help you achieve a successfully delivered complex IT project.

IT projects are always challenging, but increasing complexity means that companies face greater difficulty in ensuring that IT delivers the promised business benefits. Companies and individuals also struggle to demonstrate the direct linkages between IT investment and results. This is not only highly desirable for the organisation, it is also important for the individuals concerned; their value to their employer or customer will typically be measured by their proven impact on successful outcomes, not by effort on work in progress.

BACKDROP – UNCERTAIN TIMES

Economic uncertainty

Geo-political instability

Media confusion

Wild weather

Generation IP

Technology innovation & diversity

STILL NEED TO DELIVER ON GETTING THE JOB DONE

Despite these many challenges, others have already trodden this path and delivered beneficial results. The secret is to understand what drives these successful initiatives and follow their lead:

- Change Imperative - In IT projects, things should not be allowed to *just happen*, or be delayed or overtaken by events. Technology thrives on change, but even those most closely involved in technology and innovation, fear it. This is not the right way to achieve success. Changes must be embraced, their impact clearly evaluated and driven through in order to align, meet and deliver against business goals.

- Complexity Challenge – Delivering successful IT projects of any importance was never easy, but is now even harder. IT management is stretched in conflicting directions by resource constraints, technology advances, and business expectations. A different approach is required to avoid falling into the comfortable trap of trying to get away with simply *keeping the wheels turning,* or delaying issues in the hope that something turns up. Complexity needs to be understood and controlled.

- Strategic Drive - IT benefits are often misunderstood by those in control of the direction of the business or managing finances. To be honest, they are also often badly represented by those who are too close to the problem. To avoid the pitfalls of IT being labelled *costly and unnecessary,* the links between strategic imperatives for the business, and realities of project delivery, have to be clearly established. IT needs a strategic architecture that integrates business needs and processes with technology requirements and deliverables.

- Structured Delivery – There are many rigorous methods and methodologies available, but slavish adherence to any one is not likely to be sufficiently all-embracing, or flexible, to lead to success. Project delivery needs to be focused, well-structured, and carefully managed through an experienced blend of well-proven best practices from business and IT methodologies.

- Benefit Clarity - Results need to have recognisable and demonstrable benefits for the organisation, its competitive position and the individuals involved. Critically, the impact of investment in technology, systems, and architectures, must be explicitly linked to the actual benefits delivered. This traceability ensures that the actual and complete return on investment, and contributions of those involved, is well understood.

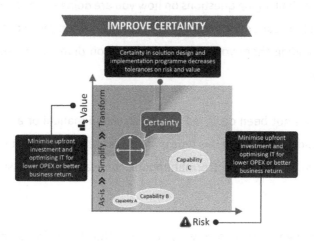

The key to this is to improve certainty of success by improving the value of the business, mitigating or managing risk, and performing sufficient upfront design and planning that takes most of the guess work out of delivery.

So, start with the end in mind. What is it that you are looking to try to achieve? Understand the need and objective of the project. You will need to document and socialise the goals and objectives of the business. Or, in other words, reach out and talk to those involved and gain their support, set them alight with the passion you have to achieve the success at the end.

This book is designed as a primer, or discussion, to provide a glimpse into how you can improve your chances of success and ask yourself challenging questions on how you are doing things currently. Many of the statements within its pages are pure common sense, and after reading them you will wonder why you didn't think about it before.

It has not been designed as an instruction manual or a step-by-step guide. If you need this type of help, please get in contact with us at www.thedigitialtransformationbook.com, as we can assist you further.

Throughout this book, we will look at the change imperative for IT, and the acceleration of change from what was experienced and expected in the 20th century in comparison to that in the 21st. We will also look at the reasons why to change, and the necessity to capture the right details so that you can communicate with everyone across the organisation in a language they will understand, yet be able to quickly adapt to change, as during the process of delivery.

We will consider the various challenges that these pose, including: technological; skill shortages; the gap between business understanding and that of IT; budget pressures; loss of control, and vested interests.

We will also provide discussion content for the imperative and strategic direction, and how the linkage between strategic direction, business architecture, systems architecture, and technology architecture can help improve the chances of your conceptual idea becoming a reality.

Various methods will be introduced to breakdown complexity; these are explained so that there is a clear way to explain the changes ahead, along with the need for them.

We will show structures in which to store the information, in order to assist in retaining the linkages; these are discussed with examples.

Also, we will provide what we believe are the key imperatives for delivering success. These are exposed, showing the characteristics or attributes believed necessary, along with questions to ask, to check if they exist in your programme and how they can apply to different initiatives.

All of the diagrams illustrated throughout this book are available in full colour on the book website at www.thedigital transformationbook.com, along with templates, personal development suggestions, free trial software, a feedback section, and lots more content.

THE CHANGE IMPERATIVE FOR IT

It is often said that the only constant is change, and projects involving the business use of IT feel this most keenly. Not only is there the incessant undercurrent of shifts and advances in the technology itself, but there are also internal and external pressures, causing business and process change across the organisation. Companies alter their focus, build partnerships, merge and spin off new structures in the face of changing economic circumstances, new legislation and competitive threats.

Sometimes planned, occasionally anticipated, but rarely easy, change can catch the most adaptable individual off guard. The reaction to imposed, unexpected, or substantial change follows a predictable path, which, without impetus, can be slow, problematic and often destructive.

While it should be possible to drive changes through from within the organisation, it is generally difficult due to the subjective proximity to the circumstances. Also, resources will already be tight, expectations will be high, and there will already be other day-to-day commitments.

External help can be vital, but crucially needs to be seen to advance, augment and support, not undermine, internal capabilities.

DEALING WITH CHANGE CURVE

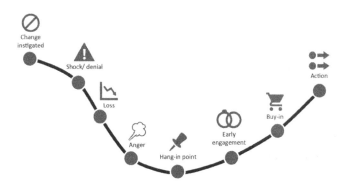

The overriding issues of changes, as perceived by those involved, usually include that it is:

- Always inevitable
- Frequently desirable
- Sometimes anticipated
- Often badly handled
- Occasionally disastrous
- Generally not managed

The key imperative for any organisation facing change, whether derived from internal plans and strategy, or imposed by external events, is to ensure that the process moves rapidly through, from resistance to positive action. This requires effective leadership and capable project management.

Project leadership is not the same as organisational leadership, or the process for managing individuals through their working career. Although there are many overlapping skills, effective project leadership is often most extensively best employed in the earliest phases of projects, with an involvement that can diminish once traditional operational management takes over. For this reason, most organisations would struggle to fully utilise this type of skillset on a permanent basis, and thus find external support both welcome and cost effective.

There is an argument that states that the old adage of *the only constant is change* has changed itself, and the new world is embracing an acceleration of change. In this new world of accelerated change, we need to become more efficient, capable, and flexible for adapting to the needs of the business in this volatile landscape, and the new evidence that is unearthed on a frequent basis. Business changing transformations that would only come about once or twice a decade, are now happening on a yearly schedule, or in some cases even more frequently.

Many organisations have spent a lot of their time improving their operational capability, such that the day-to-day work is extremely efficient, cost effective, and streamlined, using best practices such as Just-In-Time, Six Sigma, Lean, etc. This is a great achievement and means that the *business as usual* operation, when operating in a steady state, is not haemorrhaging precious resources, therefore improving its profitability and sustainability if managed correctly. This approach, with periods of instability, caused through change, coming infrequently, has been the model that companies have worked with, and is taught in business schools around the world.

Today, with major business changes occurring multiple times per year rather than per decade, organisations need to expend the same effort in changing how they transform their business, to such an end that they will make sure that these processes are equally efficient in managing time well and cost-effectively, yet flexible enough to adapt to the changing landscape in every facet of their change cycle.

Industries, standards bodies, and corporations internally have attempted to react to these phenomena through the production or modification of frameworks and methodologies, each improving on its predecessor, but none a complete answer. They represent only part of the puzzle. When these partial answers are presented for implementation, they compound the misassumption through the slavish approach to adopt one of these, which in turn can distract the organisation from the goal of improving its change capability by setting the adherence to the framework, or methodology, as the target.

These frameworks tend to be centred around a singular discipline, whether that is project management, enterprise architecture, procurement, compliance, etc., requiring and defining the touch points with the others, but not integrated. Therefore, a change in one area of the business may not be felt or reflected in another. This has ramifications on all fronts, as time and money will have been wasted; the alteration or discontinuation of the envisaged ability will probably be disheartening to the execution team performing the transformation, and the recipients expecting the new capability.

Where organisations have recognised that the *one-size-does-NOT-fit-all,* and have adopted a number of frameworks, the interfaces between each are blurred and contentious. Many create infinity loops where nothing can be delivered due to the cyclic dependencies (dependency on one process completing before another can start, yet it cannot start until its dependant has completed), or duplication of effort requiring the representation of the information in a different structure rather than viewpoint.

The concept of collaborating rather than segregating departments, projects, initiatives, etc., is seen by many as a panacea. In an attempt to make this happen, they employ vast systems with convoluted workflows to join everything together, attempting the view of a single pane of glass. If not done right, this will force teams to work in a manner that is alien to them, losing any efficiency that can be carried over from the operation, and only providing an artificial view – a shadow of the reality lurking behind it.

There should never be an IT project! All IT projects are business projects, just not necessarily with the right terminology or presented in the right way. Essentially, these business projects initiated by an IT department, fall into three categories:

1. Initiatives that will keep the business running
2. Initiatives that will reduce the operating expenditure of the business
3. Initiatives that will provide the business with a new capability

Any other justification provided is not a real reason to change, and the merits of the initiative should be scrutinised. By ensuring that the team's mind-set is firmly grounded in the needs of the business, rather than the needs of IT, the necessary works can be correctly interpreted and prioritised as any other business activity, with the correct support of the senior management team and board.

So what would come under each of the categories and how could it be interpreted?

Keep the business running projects are those covering any activity that is required to stay in business as a going concern. This may mean the adhering to new legislation or regulation, the renewal of service or licensing agreements to continue the use of existing capabilities, or the replacement of defective equipment due to general wear and tear or having gone beyond their economic useful lifespan. This category does not actively seek to improve the business operation. Nor does it introduce anything new to the organisation that could be considered a competitive advantage. In actual terms given, there is no change in an ever changing world; it can be argued that by maintaining rather than improving a capability, the organisation will experience a competitive loss, if not coupled with other innovations.

Reduce operating expenditure is exactly what it says – reducing the monthly/yearly cost to maintain the same capabilities within the organisation, at the same level of service. While this provides a reduction in cost, as with keeping the business running, it does not provide any new capabilities.

The final category is probably the most exciting, and should be the one that most businesses are striving towards. This category is the one that promotes growth in the business by inducing new capabilities. These could be:

- Automating a business process
- Simplifying communications

- Improving the engagement with the clients
- Helping support a new line of services or products
- Improving the utilisation of an asset

– and so on. It is in this final group that we can start to see the biggest differentiator between the *business as usual* mind-set, keep the lights on, and reduce operating costs and that of the transformation champion.

Given the differing nature between *business as usual* operations and business transformation, it is clear that there are equally similar differences between organisational leadership and transforming leadership. Transformational leadership is transient in nature, being brought in to life at the start of an idea, and dying at its realisation.

For this brief period, it needs to quickly and efficiently establish its own structure, separate, yet reporting to the business, not always subservient to it. It needs to operate with its own mandate, and the backing from the highest levels of the organisation, to support the changes it will make. It must be swift to take action and deliver on its promises, while being empathetic to the organisation and sympathetic to its needs. It must be clear on its vision and be able to communicate this effectively, bringing every member of the organisation along for the journey. It must be proactive in its approach, anticipating and preparing for a number of likely scenarios.

Framework in action:

"We were asked to help a large airport facilities provider, in the north west of England, with their acquisition of another airport, as their in house team did not have the correct skillset, and their big five consultancy partner didn't have expertise at the level required. This would have practically doubled their capacity and provided them with a strategic position in the south east of England, along with owning two of the major air cargo hubs in the UK.

During the initial offer pricing exercise, the general thinking was that the transition exercise to incorporate the new asset into the IT systems would take less than six months, and £2,000,000. Based on our experience, we knew this to be vastly underestimated for the size and complexity of the asset. When we challenged, it became clear that this price was plucked from thin air without any basis of fact.

They then were ready to start the journey. As the asset to be acquired was roughly the same size as their largest asset in the group, and in the same industry, we helped them build a model of their own estate, then approximated how much it would cost to amalgamate their systems. This went beyond the technology, but looked at all facets of people and processes.

This was used to create an initial bid offer to open negotiations and allow due diligence to start. In this phase, we tested the model and amended, based on information provided in the data room. It supported a team of 20 people to examine 3864 files for IT relevant content in their subject matter area, then reporting back in a comprehensive and cohesive manner.

The rich information store allowed for a detailed transition plan to be built and tested with the team IT in the acquisition. The plan proved to be robust and supported the successful winning bid for the purchase."

PRESSING BUSINESS & IT CHALLENGES

Making effective use of IT always brings complex challenges and changes to organisations, but now there are not only growing numbers of options available from technology, but also increasing commercial demands and constraints on the business. Ensuring that IT explicitly meets business needs has never been more important.

There are many items adding to the stress levels of IT projects, and most of them have little to do with the technology itself.

Far more pressing are the constraints on skills and resources, and the difficulty in articulating and linking the IT challenge to the requirements of the business.

These, coupled with any internal politics, can often undermine the control necessary to drive projects through to successful completion.

- Technology – Rapid innovation opens up opportunities, but also challenges as change impacts longer-term investment decisions. New technologies have dramatic impacts on the way everyone works, heaping further pressure on other projects. Increasing volumes, velocity and variety of information can create opportunities for new business insight, but often result in a sea of unstructured and unmanageable data.

- Skills – Recruiting, developing, and holding on to those with the right skills is a growing burden. Specialists fear being left behind in short-lived disciplines, and move to ensure their talent is best rewarded. Generalists add bulk to the budget, but can often be overwhelmed by the need for detailed expertise as projects become more complex. Balancing a workforce that can deliver in an unpredictable market and technology change conditions, has become much harder.

- Business link – Cost control is always in the IT remit, but becomes more significant when projects struggle to gain or hold support from the business. In many work places, IT and the business become entrenched in silos, where a lack of common values and communications leads to a breakdown in understanding. Both need to recognise the direct link between IT investment and the consequent value brought to the business.

- Resources – Budgets have always been tight, but all organisations are being expected to do more with less. IT is typically consumed by the fire-fighting task of keeping everything working, while at the same time facing demands for radical changes to meet new business requirements and the churn of legacy technologies. Justifying where resources will be deployed has become much more critical to survival.

- Control – The constant power struggle within organisations means that IT is often seen as simply a service provider. While it is true that IT is a business enabler and trusted partner to the business, if its control over business outcomes slips away, then the misalignment between requirements and capabilities will lead to further fragmentation; IT has to demonstrate its business value clearly and explicitly, leveraging its knowledge of how the processes and data are automated or assisted using technology. Without this, IT is in danger of being side-lined with consequent loss of influence, and ultimately budget and jobs.

- External influences – Security and privacy demands, along with increasingly onerous legislation, make it even more important to have solid procedures and good standards of governance. For many in IT this is the most daunting challenge they have faced.

Taking a wider view on the pressures and stresses that are placed on an organisation as a whole, specifically when it comes to change, you'd find that these would include:

- Achieving results
- Time
- Resource
- Budget
- Structure
- Processes
- People
- Stakeholders
- Shareholders

Those who are delivering within the IT context of the organisation should become familiar with these and how they translate to the change initiative they are undertaking. While not addressing these in the order listed, the following will hopefully outline further observations in these areas.

We can start by looking at the time pressure. As mentioned previously the need for change and the speed at which it needs to be implemented are increasing, resulting in a more flexible, agile and rapid approach to decision making is required. As an individual our decision making ability is shaped through our characteristics, cognitive biases and personal experiences. When we are put under pressure to make a decision, specifically under severe time constraints, our primitive mind is engaged, looking for patterns to match and guess the right outcome. By doing this, a fully objective and evidence based approach is less likely as the individuals judgement is influenced by intuition.

Organisations are like people in this regard, in that, with limited time available, and when all the facts are not known, decisions will be made based made on the previous experience. This experience can come from many sources: key decision makers, similar projects or initiatives, other industry examples or sought out expert opinion.

There is an argument to say that all decisions are time-bound in the sense that there is not an infinite amount of time to make a selection. And it is not the time limit that is the factor, but the quantity and quality of the information that is presented to make the decision, with the limiting factor being the time it takes to collect additional information to clarify the decision and the time it takes to analyse it. While this can happen in any organisation, it is amplified when there is an adverse or blame culture at work, by which the quantity of evidence required is proportionate to indemnify the decision being made.

There are studies published on the internet that suggest that the perception of time pressure can also impact the quality and capability of the decision making. If people believe they have ample time to come to a conclusion, they will tend to arrive at a more logically derived decision.

Taking this now in the context of a change initiative, multiple decisions are taken constantly, so an effective approach to dealing with the time pressure and information quality is required. This could include minimal information requirements, a decision making quorum and how long before a decision is made, as to make no selection is in itself a decision. There has to be acceptance that there are no wrong decisions, by changing the perception of the time pressure from being another problem to manage, to being an enabler of effective decision making, and by focusing the effort, then quickly and efficiently confirming the hypothesis.

The time saved in making the decision early can be used to test out the decision and push forward to the next stage of the change initiative. If the decision proves to be incorrect, the initiative will have found this out at the earliest possible moment, can look for alternatives and has confirmation of one route that will not work.

Once decisions have been taken, the delivery on these will form the next barrier, being the speedy delivery, which is directly affected by the iron triangle of schedule, scope and resources applied.

Information Technology, or at least the use of, is widely acknowledged to play a critical role in any organisation. This is especially true in its automation, innovation and prosperity, with more uses being found for its application. However, this has resulted in greater demand for correctly skilled, competent and capable individuals. This increased demand sees competition for these resources across the globe with the digital economy growing exponentially.

As outlined in THE CHANGE IMPERATIVE FOR IT, the skills and mind-set required to implement IT change is different from running the business. It has been estimated by the British Computer Society that the highest percentage of the IT spend is still on keeping the lights on. This clearly reinforces the need to do more with less.

Mobilising a small dedicated team, outside of the day-to-day operations, to manage, design, build and implement the changes required can be largely covered in three broad categories:

- Remove staff from their operational role and backfill. Invest in training and upskilling this team so they are equipped and able to cope with the demands of the business change and skilled to build the next business innovation; the downside being that their expertise and experience is grounded in operational delivery and not in transformational delivery.

- Outsource the initiative and subsequent management to an appropriately skilled managed service provider. This is not a silver bullet, and you can see significant knowledge attrition in the processes and automation of the business. This option does have merit when considering commodity IT services.

- Leverage outside resource while at the same time ensuring that you don't become dependent on outsourcing relationships where you can be held to ransom.

Digital Transformation

IT transformation teams are transient in nature and the structure, processes and governance need to be established quickly, along with being efficient and adaptable. This function, and the capability it brings, lives and dies with the initiative from the early moment of conception through to the benefits realisation.

Streamlining the processes and framework that the programme executes within, minimises the delays inherit with the current operating model with the associated risks of being over budget and having schedule overruns.

Ensure there is a clear mandate for the works ahead with backing and support from the senior leadership team. This should pull together the high-level strategic objectives for the programme and set the boundaries and parameters for architecting the solution. These can be developed in line with the programme vision statement through understanding the drivers behind the initiative and envisaged business goals and capabilities expected to be delivered.

Care must be taken over this stage because all partners committed to the delivery need to understand, agree and genuinely support the transformation initiative. This will be tested throughout the programmes lifespan from within the organisation that seeks to benefit from its successful conclusion; from those within the programme who are acting to deliver the capability, and externally to both. Beware of the tell-tale signs that the mandate has not been

27

clearly accepted by all, as the result will be discourse and failure to reach the goals set out from the start.

There are no IT projects, only business ones. Yet, so often an organisation sees IT as a separate entity that is *making changes to it* rather than *making changes for it*. This same attitude is perpetuated by IT departments who have opinions that the business *just doesn't understand* and *gets in the way*. This *them and us* attitude does not help in the successful delivery of a new capability, and in many cases can actively sabotage any efforts.

Bridging the gap between the business expectations and requirements to the technology capabilities and constraints must be paramount if an IT change programme is to succeed. There should be clear links and language used to identify where precious resources are being used along with when the eagerly awaited capabilities will be delivered. This should be done in a transparent manner that brings the entire organisation along on the journey, so that they can see and understand as it develops. This way, when the final delivery of the capability is performed, it is not a shock.

To see how other methodologies cater for this in the project management world, go to www.thedigitaltransformationbook.com

Framework in action:

"Coming up with a delivery plan to overhaul a large airport facilities provider for the south east of England's 12,000 users, without affecting any of the 200,000 passengers was always going to be a challenge, but one that we rose to.

As part of a £600,000,000 programme of work commissioned by the CIO we were engaged to help provide the plan, controls and architecture that could help decentralise some services for easier mergers, acquisitions or divestment, and cut operating expenses by £114,000,000 per year.

Working with Microsoft to look at the best way to consolidate services and reduce licensing costs, the plan was drafted and delivered from conception to completion in two years, allowing the objectives to be achieved."

A FLEXIBLE FOUNDATION

To avoid being overcome by the fear of driving through change, or the typical stresses facing IT projects in all organisations, a clear path needs to be set out. This is not always easy for most organisations to accomplish when everyone is caught up in the day-to-day operational requirements.

Many are put off by the perception that setting out a clear strategy will involve too much extra effort or will somehow tie them down unnecessarily, and so they continue in an ad hoc manner making tactical decisions as and when required.

In many areas of IT, the novelty of recent innovation and change are also often cited as reasons not to be pinned down to a particular approach.

This might seem as if effort and resources are being saved or protected, but the reality is that this approach will only lead to bigger issues over time.

A well thought out strategic approach needs to be taken, but the right architecture must be put in place for its support. Only then will it retain both the flexibility and the structure required to demonstrate how the strategy meets business aspirations and fits operational processes, all within the constraints of IT resources.

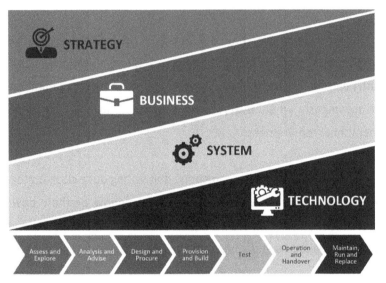

THE IMPERATIVE FOR STRATEGIC DIRECTION

- Strategic direction – A vision for the organisation that guides the development of the following architectural elements.

- Business Architecture – A description of the current and target business environments, focussing on business processes and operations.

- System Architecture – A definition of the relevant application systems that describes the applications as logical groups of capabilities, which manage information and support business processes defined above.

- Technology Architecture – The technology principles and platforms and how these provide for the needs and structure of the data and applications.

Making complex IT objectives, problems, or issues simple, is not mystical, it just needs you to apply a relevant model that helps break it down into smaller manageable collections of elements. The complex element is ensuring that this part of the whole does not get divorced from the wider initiative.

It is well documented by nearly all frameworks that solutions should be driven by the business, defined by business requirements and aligned to the overall business mission, vision and goals. This is known as top down design. Taking a top down approach helps to create the traceability back to the business that is necessary to show the value it brings.

One common complaint of this approach is that the business management teams become solely responsible for innovation and are not able to identify and assess new technology developments, translating them into business improvements. As discussed previously, these improvements need to be presented so that they represent either an operational cost saving, allowing the business to continue to be a going concern, or bring in new business.

The solution to the above is clear and simple, but its adoption is difficult for many. This isn't due to complexity, but in our experience it is down to political motivations and a lack of a common language. The solution is to accept innovation ideas where ever they arise and evaluate them in a structured manner utilising a multi-skilled, cross department team that can collaborate on articulating the goals, drivers and objectives of the proposal in a clear and well-formed approach, that is not divorced from one another and has traceability back to the core business mission, vision and objectives.

Once this information is captured in a structured way, it can be built upon and reused throughout the project and operational life of the initiative. We'll go through more about this method in the next chapter.

"So how do we get everyone to work together?" I hear you all ask. "Each department worries about different things and talks a different language!" This is where understanding how to approach creating a solution works well, and the viewpoints each will need comes into play. While not the only way of separating these, one method is to utilise the TOGAF four layer domain model.

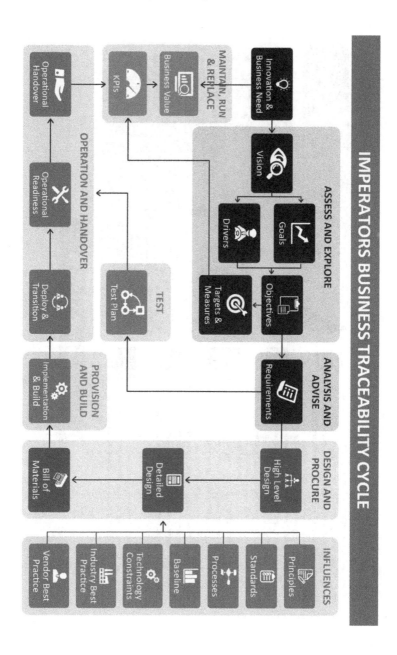

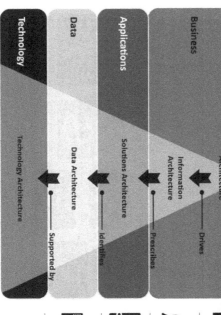

4 LAYER DOMAIN MODEL

Business — Business Architecture

Applications — Solutions Architecture

Data — Data Architecture

Technology — Technology Architecture

Information Architecture

Drives — **Prescribes** — **Identifies** — **Supported by**

Business Architecture describes the business strategy, models, processes, services and organisation. Provides the foundation upon which the other enterprise architecture dimensions base their decisions.

Information Architecture identifies documents and manages the information needs of the enterprise, assigns ownership and accountability for this information, and describes how data is stored by and exchanged between stakeholders.

Solutions Architecture defines the specification of technology enables solutions in support of the business architecture. Provides a view on how services should be bundled to support a business process.

Data Architecture defines "how" data is stored, managed and used within the enterprise and solutions. It provides the view, common guidelines and standards for data operations that make it possible to model and control data storage and give guidelines for relational databases as well as hierarchical storage.

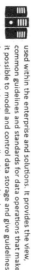

Technology Architecture defines the strategies and standards for technologies and methods used to develop, execute and operate the application architecture. It provides frameworks, technical patterns and services that support application requirements.

This proposes that the business can be split into four key areas when implementing IT.:

1. Business – This is the operating model that the business finds itself within. This can be consciously designed or unconsciously constituted through a process of natural evolution by the organisations team. Consider that it is here that the fundamental understanding for why and what the business is and does is held. How it is structured, its principles it will stand by and the processes it will work within.

   a. Information – Considered the life blood of any organisation, information is critical to its success. So the definition, accuracy, ownership, life cycle, security and flow of information is very close to the operation and transformation of any business.

It is worth observing that the above two areas exist in any organisation with or without IT. It is just the prevalence of IT as a critical component of any successful business that can tie these subjects together with the last two. In the TOGAF model, these are considered the Business Domain, but the importance of these is not to be underestimated as these are the sole reason that the underlying IT components are required.

2. Application or solution – This looks at the automation of processes and the implementation of the collaboration of information. It is common to hear this discussed as data from a technology perspective because without the right interpretation, such as the business operations view point, the information is meaningless.

3. Data – is concerned with how data is stored, managed, accessed, secured and used within the organisation and solutions.

4. Technology – the final piece of the puzzle is the technology that underpins the application. This is the incarnation of the automated processes in a form that meets the requirements of the above three areas. Here, defined, are the strategies and standards for technologies and methods used to develop, execute and operate the application architecture. It provides frameworks, technical patterns and services that support application requirements.

By understanding this model (or others), you can start to build your transformation team with clear lines of communications, with viewpoints that are relevant to their areas, using language that they can understand. Each higher layer sets out clear requirements as guidance and direction to the lower layers, while each of the lower layers presents back its recommendation to fulfil those requirements along with any constraints or standards it may have.

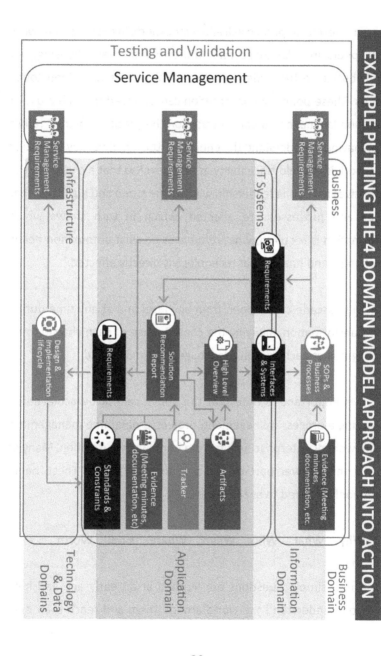

This flexible approach will allow for experts in each arena to work with peers in a language and framework of their choosing, yet contributing to the wider initiative through clearly defined touch points. These points of collaboration can be eased through a use of common language that concentrates on the specific required, rather than having to understand the entirety of the initiative. Key to making this work is to build traceability at each level so that a change in the objectives set by the leadership will *pull the string* and highlight what roles and processes are affected, which in turn shows which information is required, what references or what automation needs to change, and finally what technology is directly affected.

This cascade can happen from any level and at any time during the transformation, allowing the consequence of each change to be highlighted at each level in a language they understand.

It is important to note that the above cannot be achieved by adopting a process management, project/programme management framework or enterprise architecture framework in isolation. Many of these only answer part of the questions necessary. These being commonly referred to as the seven W's:

Why   **W**hat   **W**ho   **W**hen   **W**here   How   **W**orth

These simple questions are learned at an early age and help everyone understand the world around them and reach their own conclusions. However, the order of these questions is quite important and not always the way people would approach them.

Many books on psychology and human behaviour describe that people approach change by:

- deciding what they are going to do
- deciding how they are going to do it
- deciding when and where
- deciding how much it is going to cost (or worth)
- then finally, deciding on a reason why they are doing it.

This method can lead to a lot of time wasted on investigating ideas that have no meaningful value or a very link back to a plausible and achievable benefit.

What is needed is to understand the reasoning up front and change the way people approach innovation and initiatives. Making the order of questions as presented above, Peter Drucker stated that "Management is doing things right; leadership is doing the right things."

How we ask these questions and the reason behind it is also important. A journalist will ask the same questions, for a different reason, to a consultant or business leader. Therefore, consider the following:

Why do we want to do this? – What is the motivation behind this innovation or initiative. Does it tie into the three key reasons to change (save money, continue to operate, support new product/service)? What business goal or driver does it address? Does it align to the corporate values and principles?

You may seek answers to these questions from the leadership, communications business plan, culture of the organisation and change plan.

What is it that we are trying to achieve? Or **What** is it we are doing? – Clearly defined articulation of what will change and how it links back to the business objectives or other identified business need.

This should be put across as a high level strategy, seeking permission to proceed with an early and high level amount of details. It should not be a *fait-accompli*. Consider that this can be set at a corporate level, business unit or product/service level but must show traceability back to the business objectives.

Who is going to be involved? – is this something that will affect the entire organisation, or just a subset? Is this purely internal, or will it be visible externally to customers, suppliers, and competitors? Is there any government or other regulatory body involvement or notification required? How will this be viewed by each of these groups?

When will we be doing this? – Are there any key trigger points? Are there any constraints such as regulatory compliance? Have we made any public promises such as customers having something ready by a specific time? Or internal promises as to not affect company morale? Are there any key dependencies that could delay the realisation of this initiative?

Perhaps you should consult the existing strategic plan, annual plan or other programme or project management forecast.

Where is this going to happen? – This could be closely linked to the **Who** question in the locations that these people are present. It could also be a question about target markets, distributor or distribution capability, leveraging outsourcing or other As-a-Service models.

How is this going to happen? – This really comes down to the planning aspects. Starting with broad strokes at the high level key activates or phases, then building up to include the minutiae, if required. This should also include communication planning, adoption plans, training and support. How are you going to measure success? There are too many multi-million initiatives sitting in corporate garden sheds because they didn't take into account how it will be operated once implemented.

Worth – is the final step and is more than just how much it will cost. It should cover the value that the initiative will bring to the business and also show what the cost will be if it is NOT done.

It is worth pausing for a moment to reflect on the previous sentence regarding **Worth**, in by NOT doing something, there are as many consequences as there is in doing something. Inaction in itself is an action, like so many things in a business, just because the action, role, or decision is not explicitly done with mindful and active commitment, or, implicitly done without full consideration or relevant due-diligence, does not mean it will not have an effect either positive or negative.

There is no right or wrong answer to this one as there is a time and place for both. The main thing is to be conscious that it is happening and be aware of what evidence and risk you are willing to accept.

Make sure you are actively answering the right question for the business. It is easy to fall into the trap of addressing the wrong issue or trying to justify a course of action or technology without a sound reason to do so. By working through the questions as presented above, you will hopefully have a good method to *sanity check* the initiative.

When doing this, do this as broadly as possible. Once you have targeted the right question, think a bit more laterally and see which of the other questions should be answered too. The level of detail will vary, but you want to be as comprehensive as the time and budget allows. The above flow of questions help a hypothetical project actually cover a lot of ground quickly, without burning a lot of resources.

Read more about Enterprise Architecture methodologies at www.thedigitaltransformationbook.com.

Framework in action:

"Sometimes you just don't know what you don't know, and that was the position a large European electronic payments provider. They knew they wanted to move faster, with less problems, rework and duplicated costs, but couldn't get a process to work with the existing teams.

On this occasion, we weren't there to do, but to help the existing team identify the gaps, skill up, and do it for themselves.

This consultancy and mentoring engagement cover a number of IT areas including: enterprise architecture methodology, process, and working. It included explicit enterprise architecture department lead mentoring, IT service management conception to implementation planning and coaching, application lifecycle platforms conception to implementation guidance and project delivery.

An example of the impact was clearly demonstrated by cutting the major incident failover process from a 60 minute downtime, to 15 minutes, through nothing other than process changes and role empowerment."

STRUCTURED APPROACH

As we have outlined so far, the information that is gathered and used is precious and important, so when it comes to its recording and reutilisation, there are a couple of key aspects that we have found to work time and time again.

Whether you are involved in a merger, acquisition or divestment; consolidating or aligning disparate business units, delivering business transformation or service transformation, potentially looking at IT function change, or gaining capabilities at the business level, the information should be collected along with the structural and descriptive information that allows for it to be categorised and associated with other elements.

For a very basic example, something that appears as a business goal, such as: increasing sales by 50%, would be linked to more specific objectives such as acquiring 10 new customers per month. That could be expressed as a more detailed requirement such as ensuring all sales leads are recorded centrally into a singular database and contact maintained on a weekly basis. Each goal would have multiple objectives; each objective would have multiple requirements. But should a constraint mean that a requirement cannot be met, then it would be clear which objectives and goals would be affected.

This approach is not new, and forms the basis of both scientific and medical practices. From a medical perspective, this evidence-based design is the conscientious, explicit and judicious use of current best evidence in making decisions about the care of individuals, when viewed from a medical point of view. Hopefully you can see clearly why this idea is so powerful and how it transfers nicely to the practice of transforming IT delivery.

It is data-driven, meaning that the approach and action is built off of the information collected and understood, compelled by data rather than by some vague intuition, gut feeling or personal experience. This does not mean the procrastination of *Analysis Paralysis,* where by decisions are delayed or postponed on every increase amount of information demanded to make decisions from, but taken as per the Pareto principle, otherwise known as the 80:20 rule, with clear understanding of the keys points, such that 20% of the information will direct 80% of the actions.

Therefore, at the core of any initiative, we advocate a strong use of both data driven modelling and an evidence based approach.

But, what does this mean in reality, and where do we start? If you have any background in systems design, whether IT or otherwise, then the following will be very familiar.

You start by mapping out the high level steps in your process in regards to what information informs or affects another. This could be done top down from strategy or direction of the organisation, or bottom up from the systems, technologies, and features. In fact, the most useful and rich data sets that we have worked with utilise both of these methods.

What are *Top Down* or *Bottom Up* methodologies? *Top down* describes a process of decomposing an idea from its highest, most all-encompassing form, such as *increase the bottom line by 20%,* to the individual actions and systems (and sub systems) that will be put in place to achieve this; Whereas *bottom up* examines each of these sub systems and tasks, piecing them together into a complex system or representation of the high level we stated earlier. This could be the adding together of rich market information with contact management, with an eager sales team and automated document creation for pitches and proposals, to allow the sales force to be more productive in selling rather than administration.

If we take a closer look at an example, we can consider the Strategy Development and Road Mapping diagram below:

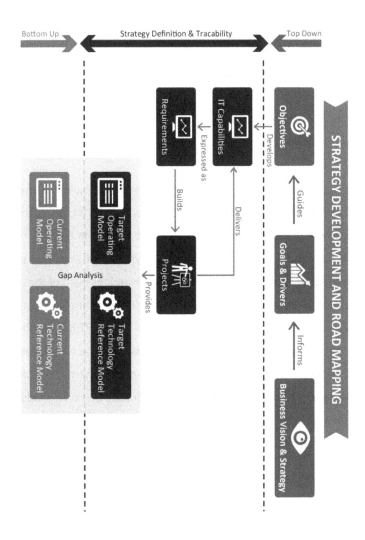

Here you can see illustrated the flow of information that affects planning from both the top down and bottom up vantage points. Breaking this down in a decomposing model, it would be described from the top down as:

1) Understand and document the business strategy and vision

2) Utilise the business strategy to inform what the company wants to achieve (its goals), and why it wants to achieve these (its drivers). This is more detailed than the strategy and vision, but not detailed enough to deliver.

3) Guided by these goals and drivers, are the objectives – a specific series of results that a person or system aims to achieve within a time frame and with available resources. In general, objectives are more specific and easier to measure than goals. Objectives are basic tools that underlie all planning and strategic activities. They serve as the basis for creating policy and evaluating performance. Some examples of business objectives include: minimizing expenses, expanding internationally, making a profit. These all should confirm to the SMART criteria in that they are:

   a. Specific
      i. Target a specific area for improvement.
      ii. Is the objective precise and well-defined? Is it clear? Can everyone understand it?

b. Measurable

    i.   Quantify, or at least suggest an indicator of progress.

    ii.   How will the individual know when the task has been completed? What evidence is needed to confirm it? Have you stated how you will judge whether it has been completed or not?

c. Attainable

    i.   Assuring that an end can be achieved.

    ii.   Is it within your capabilities? Are there sufficient resources available to enable this to happen? Can it be done at all?

d. Relevant

    i.   State what results can realistically be achieved, given available resources.

    ii.   Is it possible for the individual to perform the objective? How sensible is the objective in the current business context? Does it fit into the overall pattern of work?

e. Time Based

    i.   Specify when the result(s) can be achieved.

    ii.   Is there a deadline? Is it feasible to meet this deadline? Is it appropriate to do this work now? Are there review dates?

4) These objectives are then used to develop and describe the capabilities that are required to meet the objectives; or, to put it another way, the abilities required to perform or achieve certain actions and outcomes as described in the objectives, through a set of controllable and measurable faculties, features, functions, processes and services.

5) These capabilities are described as functional (what it does), and non-functional (what it is), requirements.

   a. Functional requirements describe what the system should do, its behaviours, inputs and outputs. Generally, these are the direct representation of the objectives in sufficient detail to allow development of the system required.

   b. Non-functional requirements are generally more operational in the perspective of looking at behaviours. Where there are a number of qualities that can be outlined, some that can be considered include:

      i.   Usability – look & feel, lingual, disability.

      ii.   Performance – response times.

      iii. Scalability – volumes, transaction throughput, extensibility.

      iv.   Availability & Recoverability – normal system operation, uptime, data integrity, system and data restoration, disaster recovery.

v. Supportability – support, technical support, coverage, training.

vi. Maintainability – planned maintenance, upgrades, change management.

vii. Security – access, authentication, authorisation, protection, policies, auditing.

viii. Standards – architecture and design covering: software, platform, virtualisation, data storage, backup, monitoring, integration, open standards, infrastructure services, network services.

ix. Legal / Regulatory – regulatory, legality, data protection, health & safety.

6) These requirements can then be collected into logical units of work to deliver unique products, services or results back into the organisation in the form of change deliverables, delivered through projects.

7) During the planning phase of the project, these deliverables can be outlined or expressed as a Target Operating Model and a Target Technology Reference Model.

a. The Target Operating Model, or TOM, describes the operation of the business as it will be at the end of the change. This usually includes: processes, capabilities, roles, responsibilities, accountabilities, organisational structure, incentives, locations, vendors, business partners, systems, IT and other assets necessary to deliver the services required.

b. The Target Technology (or technical) Reference Model, or TRM, outlines the technology building blocks (or sub systems) that make up the solution to help deliver the system with the services as described in the TOM. It will describe each of the components and conceptual structure for the IT system, or its taxonomy, along with its association with the other components in an ontology, describing their relationships such as providers and consumers or dependants and suppliers, or successors and predecessors, effectively mapping out potential pre-requisites in the technology estate.

8) The gap analysis between what already exists, to what is envisaged, forms the change tasks to achieve the outcomes outlined in the projects.

If the above process is followed, then there is a rich volume of information that can be utilised throughout the transformation cycle to help report on progress and advise of direction. However, what happens when the strategy changes?

From here, patterns can be identified through the appropriate categorisation of the information held that can assist in decomposing the whole into manageable deliverables. As the old saying goes, *you eat only an elephant one mouthful at a time.*

It is important to note though that the information is only as good as what is put in, along with who has assessed and compiled it. As with any information management system, without the engagement of the right people, with the relevant experience within the organisation and skillset, there is a risk of *garbage in, garbage out* being the result.

Life is change, and the dogmatic adherence to the delivery of a plan set months, if not years, in advance will only result in a product or service that is no longer required, and at the expense of the two most valuable resources the organisation has – time and money!

This is clear, and will be self-evident, if you look in your own organisation:

- How many projects have been delivered on-time and to budget, according to the original plan?
- How many of those projects changed during their life cycle?
- How many of those projects didn't live up to the organisations expectations?

I have yet to find anyone who can provide positive answers to any of these questions when being honest with themselves.

One of the key reasons for this is that through the delivery of the project, and the elapsed time of the organisation, further information is brought to light that changes the original premise that the planning directions were made on. For many, this new information cannot be folded back into the rich data set to understand its upwards or downwards impacts because the data set is divorced from each other. Or in other terms, there is no traceability. You cannot pull on the string of a capability to work out what part of the strategy it is delivering, or what requirement is directly delivering it.

Therefore, building a model whereby each discrete piece of information interrelates with others, both more abstract and more detailed, will allow you to assess quickly what is affected with each change. We can see this in action when you consider the capability development cycle on page 58.

It takes its founding direction from the business strategy, culture enterprise vision, direction, corporate social responsibility, and environmental concerns, using these to develop the guiding principles that will govern and inform the operation and transformation of the organisation.

Martin Sharp & Edward Johns

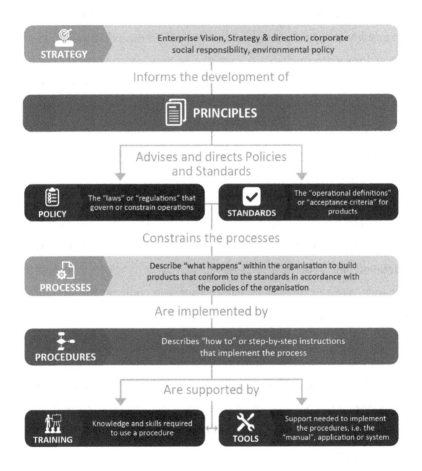

These are then used to inform the development of policies (the *laws* or *regulations* that govern or constrain operations) and standards (the *operational definitions* or *acceptance criteria* for products), which, in turn, both constrain the processes, and provide focus for those that are required.

These processes describe *what happens* within the organisation to build products that conform to the standards in accordance with the policies of the organisation, are implemented into executable flows of work in procedures, describing *how to* or *step-by-step* instructions that implement the process.

To automate, or assist in accomplishing the processes, tools can be implemented to work in the system, as support needed to implement the procedures. For example, the *working manual,* application or system.

Working within a system that is unknown will not yield the positive results envisaged in the business strategy, so training needs to be provided, imparting knowledge and skills required to use a procedure.

If a change is introduced at any point in this cycle, and the relevant linkages exist between the elements shown, its impact can be quickly identified and the relevant risk mitigation and management steps started.

Your next steps to implement something similar are:

1. Define your Methodology
2. Adopt a Data Modelling Approach
3. Ensure Alignment and Traceability

If you are not sure what tool set to start with, look at our recommendations for collaborating on your next initiative by going to www.thedigitaltransformationbook.com.

Framework in action:

"This client was a regulated company whose charges were set five years in advance, based on the predicted sales and investments being made.

–Working in both roles as programme director and lead architect for the definition of the IT Infrastructure strategy, including creating a data model to capture as-is and to-be with traceability through to business objectives. This data model was utilised by a team of eight subject matter experts to capture and analyse the findings.

–Taking an evidence based approach, including primary and secondary research capturing, current inflight and planned projects along with known business cases and themes. Cumulated in a technology strategy, delivery blueprint and programme definition of £101m delivered in six months, and still used as the foundation for planning activities at the time of writing."

DELIVERING SUCCESS

For IT projects, it is no longer sufficient to measure success based on *in time, in budget* (as if they were all achieving this in any event!). There has to be a direct and credible connection between investment and results. This requires an approach that combines a number of elements within frameworks that can be employed and adapted to suit different types of projects.

We examined many projects that we delivered, as well as those delivered by others, along with successes and failures. From this, we believe that the following attitudes and actions, or imperative, from the delivery team and management team members, are critical as the seed for success.

- Lead – effective leadership through change
- Align – business goals and IT
- Clarify - impact and responsibilities of all parties
- Connect - business, system and technology elements
- Sharpen - focus on objectives and outcomes
- Structure - reporting for maximum comprehension
- Support – the process once underway

These cannot be taken in isolation, but embraced as a whole, with each supporting the other to achieve the success required.

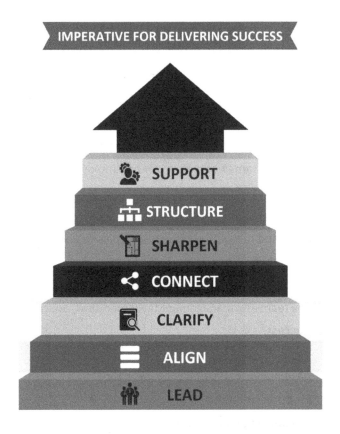

A positive attitude has been proven by many to be the catalyst to success. With a positive attitude, you no longer wallow in the problems or perpetuate the issues, but look for the positives, the learnings, and the solutions. When building your team, you will already be looking out for members who have this characteristic.

Attitude is only half of the equation; without action, nothing will happen. It is by acting on those learnings, solutions and ideas, that you will move forward. This is not only a business phenomenon but is seen in all areas of life. If you want to change the colour of your wall, it won't paint itself.

But what actions should be taken? What if it isn't obvious what the solutions are, or what learning you should be acting on?

There are some simple questions that you can ask yourself, aligned to the imperatives, that can help you identify these next steps:

Attitudes	Questions	Imperatives
Lead through change	Are your projects over budget or over time? Are you struggling to gain business support?	Lead through strategic definition and architecture.
Alignment and traceability	Are your project stakeholders complaining? Have you no traceability to business goals and objectives?	Align business goals and IT
Clarity & Clarify	Is your project governance unclear? Is your benefit path unclear?	Clarify - impact and responsibilities of all parties

Attitudes	Questions	Imperatives
Consequential Connection	Is the operational workload constraints or recurring problems? Do you have no link from investment to business benefit?	Connect business, system and technology elements
Sharpen Focus	Is your focus drifting, or delivery slipping? Are the interdependencies and structure challenging to communicate?	Sharpen focus on objectives and outcomes
Strategic Structure	Are the project priorities unclear? Are you drowning in valuable but unstructured information or data?	Structure reporting for maximum comprehension
Support	Are the internal expertise lacking? Are your teams overburdened?	Support the process once underway

This pattern has already been used in various ways for different types of projects, each with the same intended outcome, driven to successful completion by providing clear and demonstrable value to the business, with traceable linkage to the resources involved at each stage.

- Planning – Have business needs been fully understood and an actionable and flexible plan put in place that will deliver them? Critically, complexity and cost should be well understood and under control as these most often undermine IT projects.

- Delivery – The link between benefit and investment needs to be absolutely clear, and interdependencies well understood and clearly documented. Only by adopting a structured approach can success be achieved.

- Recovery – Already off-track, out of scope, over budget or over time? Focus and momentum that has been lost can be regained by employing firm direction and leadership. Objective decisions need to be taken and structure re-applied.

- Business integration – This might be the re-alignment of different business units, mergers and acquisitions, or simply IT *sprawl*. It is vital to understand the scale of the challenge, risk profile, and executive support, and then plan to keep control of costs and minimise user impact.

- Business transformation – Often driven by the relationship between the business and IT, services not based on business need or able to change as those needs evolve, or there might be a complete disconnection between the two. Dependencies need to be understood and firmly managed, and resources freed up to be more effectively deployed. Strong and dispassionate leadership is required.

While the above theory sounds great, where people trip up is in its applications. The following page shows some example Imperatives for Integration and Transformation.

Initiative	Imperatives
Mergers and Acquisitions	Continued operation, smart sourcing and partner selection Rapid transition and integration, cost and risk control
Disparate Business Units	Building consensus, rapid re-alignment, clear deliverables Focus, control, project acceleration, early benefits
Business Transformation	Support and agreement, IT and business aligned Smooth *step-changes*, improved internal dialogue
Service Transformation	Improved contract control and partner management Clarity of service, performance and delivery
IT Function Change	Boost internal experience and skillsets Grow business agility and flexibility
Gaining Capabilities	Process automation, fully representative data models New working practices, productivity boost

Measure yourself and your current project against these traits by downloading the Significant 7 Imperatives Maturity Model from www.thedigitaltransformationbook.com.

Framework in action:

"When purchasing a divested asset, it can be complicated to understand what you have purchased and what you will end up with, and from an IT perspective can be a significant challenge. When you are talking about divesting and amalgamating private hospitals to create a new company with over 30 locations, the ramifications for getting it wrong could be life shattering for those in their care.

Working with the acquiring and divesting parties to understand what was included in the purchase, and what the original system entailed, it was clear there were going to be some big gaps that required thought leadership rather than a traditional transition and transformation model.

A new model was created centring on the transition of data and the on-site equipment. This would be implemented into a centralised infrastructure, geographically dispersed for resilience but utilising all the capabilities and capacity available, while at the same time allowing all doctors, nurses, consultants, and other medical and administrative personnel, access wherever they were to the information they needed to do their job.

This new way of working preceded most private and public clouds but provided the same level of flexibility with security, and could only be accomplished through the alignment of objectives to the business goals and support from every level within the organisations involved.

The resultant service was delivered on-time, below budget, and with a richer capability than was originally expected."

DEMONSTRABLE BREADTH OF VALUE

Many people talk about benefits, when they are really referring to improvements or advantages, but these are not things that have clear and tangible business value. Advantages may have benefits attached, but to be converted into actual benefits, they need to be linked to the value that is derived. Two primary axis can be used for outlining benefits, which can be categorised into financial versus operational, and increasing versus decreasing. Essentially, something can increase *value add* or flexibility, otherwise it can reduce cost or risk.

For example, a new system might *speed things up*, but if there is no financial or operation saving or gain, the value cannot be quantified. Both financial and operational benefits are directly linked to the performance of the business, and so provide a traceable and direct link to something that can be widely recognised.

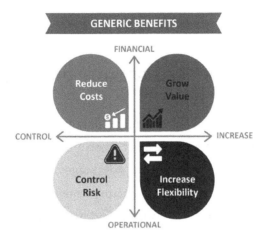

However, value or benefit, in the case of an IT project, should not be limited to the impact it has on the organisation, but should also include other considerations to understand the complete impact.

Firstly, consider the individual or individuals responsible for the project. These people are critically involved; crucially, their future standing in the organisation, and beyond, will depend on the level of success or otherwise of the project. This sounds fair, but all too often there is a lack of clarity between objectives as understood by the wider business, and the technical goals set, as part of the project. Those running the project may believe they have accomplished what was required, but that is not how it is perceived. It is in their personal interests for this to be more focused and better understood.

There are also external considerations to take into account. An organisation might pat itself on the back for delivering what was apparently a successful project, only to find out that this still leaves it substantially behind its competitors.

Similarly, it might take a dim view of another project that appeared to miss its internal goals, but leapfrogs the competition, or greatly improves the relationship with an influential external partner or client.

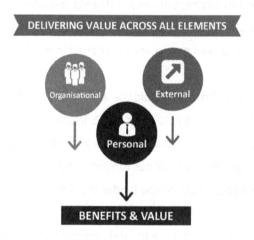

All of these considerations need to be built in from the outset in a way that captures the wider beneficial impact and links the investment decisions at each stage to the business results actually delivered. Those directly involved may be able to do this, but often an external viewpoint, that is more emotionally detached, can more easily capture the bigger picture and ensure that the right connections are made.

It is an unfortunate fact of human nature that, for many, value starts with a personal view of *what's in it for me?* and means that, for many, they won't commit what is required, even if it is the right action, if there are ill consequences for their position. This is a primal instinct and well documented in Maslow's hierarchy of needs.

By clearly articulating and demonstrating the benefits and values for the individual, you have a higher likelihood of success, as the individuals in focus will have a vested interest in making it happen.

The inverse is also true, should the individual deem that the action or initiative be detrimental to their needs in any form such as loss of position, loss of respect, isolation, removal from peer group, risk of position, risk of security or other fundamental drivers, causing that person to sabotage or otherwise hinder the progress.

Therefore, ensuring a clear and understandable path where objectives are defined and can be followed, and that pay attention to the persons needs at an individual level, as well as a group, is important to success.

Organisation benefits and values are paramount to any delivery. In most cases, these are the most concentrated on, as they are the key goals and drivers behind the change. However, they are not always well articulated into a form that makes it clear what *good* looks like.

As previously mentioned, there are only three reasons to change:

1. Initiatives that will keep the business running
2. Initiatives that will reduce the operating expenditure of the business
3. Initiatives that will provide the business with a new capability to generate income

When you examine these three reasons, you will hopefully see that the first two are clearly drivers, or what the business is trying to avoid or move away from, while the third is a goal, or something the business wants to move towards or obtain.

Understanding this simple definition will aid greatly when it comes to articulating the organisational benefit or value. Consider a way to collaborate more closely with your clients. If we examine this under each of the three reasons for change, you will see different and distinct messages being drawn:

- Keep the business running: being able to service our clients is paramount, and the sharing of information is crucial for that success. Without it, we will no longer be able to service our clients.

- Reduce operational expenditure: improving the speed and ease in which we exchange information with our clients will reduce the amount of unproductive time and allow for faster turnaround of work.

- Generate income: collaborating quicker and easier with our clients will improve the speed of response and the ability to get through more work quickly, allowing us to reduce costs, increase throughput, and to show a marketable advantage.

Knowing who the recipient of the information is, and what they are looking for, is key. Those who are concerned with moving away from the current problems will clearly be more enamoured by a driver statement while those with an eye on the future will be looking for goal statements.

It is not easy with a mixed audience, but, ensuring you have both types covered, you are more likely to appeal to both sets of individuals.

You can express these benefit statements in terms of reduced cost and increased control, which, as we have now illustrated, is a driver towards better control; or grow value and increase flexibility, which is a goal of increasing value.

The methods that these use to achieve and measure the benefit are different though. Reduced costs and grow value have fiscal indicators, whereas control risk and increase flexibility are operationally focused in either increasing the quantity of control and process, or decreasing it accordingly.

Thinking about the external benefits and value is probably the most difficult, but in many cases is the most important. The external parties that are affected by this change could be clients, customers, governing bodies, trade associations, peers, competitors, candidates, governments, or, in fact, anyone that is affected directly or indirectly.

I believe it is fair to say that there is a lot of focus from organisations when developing services that will be consumed by its customers or clients, especially if that is a key revenue stream. But consider also the others that form part of the eco-system. If you generate a fantastic change that your clients love, but is illegal in the country you are in, you will probably find yourself in a painful position with your government. While this is an extreme example, I hope it helps provide a good illustration, as it could easily apply to governing bodies or accrediting bodies, trade associations or others who provide standards or codes of conduct.

Thinking about the impact on your peers or trading partners can be an interesting experiment. Consider if you obtain 20% of your income from a business partner, but could easily recreate the service they offer. Would you? What would be the impact? You could probably undercut them, but then you would also lose their client base, or at least have to compete for it. You'd have to keep updating the service or product to stay ahead, or they will return to your ex-partner who will probably be working with someone else. These are just a few thoughts on the external impact you could be having.

Framework in action:

"When it was obvious to our client that their £440,000 IT project, that was part of a multibillion pound infrastructure change, was in trouble of coming in late, we were asked in to help – especially since the announcement of the opening date had been global news and was only months away.

It was clear that while the major assets had clear and demonstrable value chains, the IT streams had been carved up into components, to which the vendors had created their own little thiefdoms. Without a clear design or clear plan, each vendor became its own warring party in a blame game of who was responsible for the delays.

The design of how to integrate these disparate components, and a plan to manage the bickering competitors, was required; but this had to be done in flight so called for some agile working methods.

A clear understanding of the value of each component was collected and collated along with the integration needs. These were captured and fed into an overarching design. A plan to deliver the integration, along with adequate testing, was devised along with making all parties co-operate through the establishment of a number of working groups, hosted on behalf of the end client, and chaired to force agreements.

The result was the services launched on time."

DELIVERING REAL BENEFITS

IT projects can often appear to be managed successfully to completion, and yet no one is really happy. Work has been done, resources deployed and budgets met, but, without the firm connections of accomplishment to specific benefits for the business, the value will not be recognised, and, in many cases, probably has not really been properly delivered. It is no wonder that those who make financial commitments and decisions often deride IT projects as either too expensive or unnecessary.

It does not need to be this way.

Organisations can deliver changes today that provide real business benefits, but this process must be driven by business need and with full understanding of the elements involved, by both IT and the business.

By taking a systematic and strategic approach, clear, understandable, and relevant benefits can be delivered to the business as it stands today, or by what can be achieved for tomorrow:

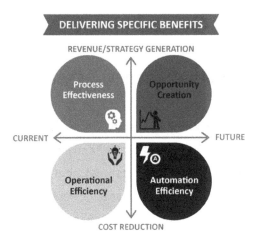

- Process Effectiveness – By understanding the existing business environment and what it would look like if improved, processes can be optimised to be much more effective. This requires an analysis of the capabilities required to perform these processes, and the kinds of application systems that would be necessary to provide those capabilities. The outcome is a streamlining of business processes, tightly coupled with the systems required to support them, making them able to deliver more.

- Operational Efficiency – In a similar vein, but looking for optimisation in the operational systems that support business processes, improvements can be made by investigating the technology architecture, and creating a better fit to the application systems that are relevant to the enterprise. Can data be re-distributed to be more effective? Could cloud-based services bring in flexibility? Can hardware be rationalised? The outcome should be cost and risk reduction by having the right technology to underpin the systems required by the business.

- Automation Efficiency – With a view to future improvement, automation of existing manual or cumbersome technology solutions can reduce costs. Examples include the deployment of mobile technologies or increased use of virtualised environments. However, the gains promised in any of these areas can be dramatically compromised without suitable strategic direction, as many have discovered.

- Opportunity Creation – Taking a strategic view of the business, rather than the technology, allows for new initiatives to be undertaken and new revenues generated. However, planning such a step needs a solid understanding of the risks, a way to resolve interdependencies and challenges from the existing structure, as well as a clear way forward. If the benefits of new endeavours fail to materialise quickly, or it is not clear where they have come from, initiatives are often deemed to have failed, when in reality the link between action and result has not been correctly attributed.

IT and business projects can deliver immediate and relevant benefits, but only if changes are driven, the organisation is internally correctly aligned, and a strategic, clear, and well-understood architecture is in place. The imperative for IT is to embrace this approach and work with those who know how to make it a reality.

There is a fifth category of real value, that being Maintaining operations – Keep the business running as mentioned, covering any activity that is required to stay in business as a going concern. This may mean adhering to new legislation or regulation, renewal of service or licensing agreements to continue the use of existing capabilities, or replacement of defective equipment due to general wear and tear or being beyond their economic useful lifespan. This category does not actively seek to improve the business operation. Nor does it introduce anything new to the organisation that could be considered a competitive advantage. In actual terms given, there is no change in an ever changing world; it can be argued that by maintaining rather than improving a capability, the organisation will experience a competitive loss, if not coupled with other innovations.

In the previous chapter, we introduced the concept benefits from different viewpoints – personal, organisational and external – as part of understanding the breadth of value being delivered. Now we will consider some of the specific real benefits for each of these categories as they are shown through the lens of cost, value, risk and flexibility.

From an organisational standpoint, the more common aspects could include:

Costs:

- Efficient and cost effective IT – these are very subjective depending on the industry you are in and the size of organisation you are. But one simple fact remains paramount – *best in class* is not always necessary; *good in class* could be what is required. When we talk about *good in class*, you are looking for a product or service that you believe the vendor will be around to support for some time to come, has a vested interested in its continual growth and support, along with meeting all of the core functional and non-functional requirements. This could mean going for a lower level leader or challenger from Gartner's Magic Quadrant because it may be easier to implement or integrate in your environment, or you already have the capability to use and support it.

- Lower cost IT procurement – striking a good deal with your vendors over any procurement is paramount, and having a good team who can find and negotiate these deals is key. But don't be too fast to wield the demand too much, as the savings you make today could cost you tomorrow in poor service or higher costs on other items. Try to have a transparent relationship with your key vendors so you both see clearly that there is a win-win opportunity.

- Faster, simpler IT procurement – negotiating, and renegotiating, IT procurement contracts through proposals, quotes and tendering processes, is a time consuming job. In many cases, this time could be better spent elsewhere, and the money saved on the product or service may have been spent on the people dealing with the purchase – a so called *penny wise, pound foolish* strategy. Therefore, setup transparent agreements with key vendors and review these periodically, and don't forget to test the market occasionally to ensure that you are still receiving the value you expect.

Value:

- Better linkage to business objectives – there should be no project that is started without a clear link to a business objective. These could be in the form of the previously mentioned three key reasons to change, if they haven't further been defined by your organisation – continue viability, reduce cost or increase revenue.

- Maximised return on exiting IT investments – sweating assets or over committing workloads are commonplace methods of trying to increase the return on investment, but many organisations purchase IT products or services and then only use a small percentage of its capability. Perhaps you should review what you have purchased and see if you can put to use those additional items. You never know; they may just help reduce cost or increase revenue by delivering better flexibility or capability.

- Improved business capability – if you provide a new capability to an organisation that can then capitalise on it to generate revenue or reduce costs, you have clearly delivered value.

Risk:

- Reduced risk on future IT investments – having to switch services or migrate between products is expensive and a drain on both time and resources. Consider the longevity of a product, service, and vendor before making the purchase. Also, think about how it will fit in with the remainder of your IT eco-system. Buying something because it has a cheap ticket price could mean an expensive management overhead, or increased risk of data loss or corruption.

- Reduced business risk from IT – IT is a great set of tools, but like any box of tools it should be used appropriately. Just like you wouldn't use a hammer to fit a glass pane, don't use the wrong IT product or service to mitigate a business risk; you are more likely to increase the risk or decrease the time it takes to realise the risk.

- Reduced critical architecture and failure points – this is all about recoverability, reliability and security. Make sure that your data is safe, tells you when there is a problem, tries to correct itself. and can be retrieved if lost.

Flexibility:

- For business growth or restructuring – while no one has a 100%, foolproof fortune teller they can consult with, having a good idea of how the business will change over the next five to ten years will help you make the right decisions. If you believe that the business will venture into multinational markets, then perhaps seek cloud services that can work well in all global locations as an example.

- For opportunities for mergers or acquisitions – You want it to be simple to prune or graft organisational units. For example, if you know there is a desire to sell off a number of business units over the next six years, moving to a centralised strategy may not be the best idea, as the cost to divest the asset will increase dramatically, therefore decreasing its value.

- Better business agility – the ability to change rapidly to capitalise on changes in the marketplace is a key driver in business in the 21st century. Building your IT on traditional inflexible models can stunt your growth, and even challenge your existence.

- Better integration, portability, and interoperability – tied closely to agility, the ability to connect disparate services or products together to share information either internally or with clients with a powerful asset. This can be used as the building blocks to further automation and efficiencies.

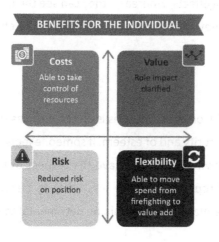

Now consider the personal benefits on the same dimensions, example of such could include:

Costs:

- Able to take control of resources – people can measure their own success in the number of people they manage, or size of the budget they control, or value of the project they've delivered. The ability to control resources provides them with significance within their peer group.

Value:

- Role impact clarified – understanding the value that an individual delivers gives them a sense of purpose. When someone doesn't believe the role they are performing is worthwhile, it has detrimental effects, whereas if they can see the positive impact it is having, they will continue, if not increase the efforts applied.

Risk:

- Reduced risk on position – this is one that drives the basic primal needs of security and of esteem. If someone feels that they are in a secure environment and have the respect of their superiors, peers and reports, they are less likely to become anxious or behave in a manner that would be detrimental to the initiative.

Flexibility:

* Able to move spend from firefighting to value add – no one likes firefighting, yet in many organisations this feels like the norm. Moving to a position where you feel you are adding value improves your feeling of self-worth, and, in turn, improves your willingness to add further value.

Templates to help you maintain traceability are available on the books website at www.thedigitaltransformationbook.com.

Framework in action:

"The quality and integrity of information is critical for any company. But when your company's major asset is the information, such as study data for pharmaceuticals, it is paramount that it is handled with care and a clear chain of custody that meets GAMP best practice, and will be acceptable to regulatory bodies.

When dealing with a highly complex and politically charged asset exchange between two pharmaceutical giants, the need to provide the right structure and leadership to gather the relevant information within the IT systems landscape, develop a target architecture and operating model, along with a transition plan, is key.

Moving from the feasibility and design phases into implementation and execution, the roles involved establishing and managing a governance framework to support the operations teams, while, at the same time, linking clearly back to tangible benefits and being flexible to adapt to changing conditions that were being put in place by either party."

THE SIGNIFICANT 7 IMPERATIVES
FOR ALL IT PROJECTS

Throughout this book we have outlined the change imperative for IT, the acceleration of change from what was experienced and expected in the 20th century in comparison to that in the 21st, the reasons why to change, and the necessity to capture the right details so that you can communicate with everyone across the organisation in a language they will understand, yet be able to quickly adapt to change as during the process of delivery.

So what is an imperative?

Oxford English Dictionary defines imperative as an adjective: *"Of vital importance; crucial"* or *"Giving an authoritative command; peremptory"* and, as a noun: *"An essential or urgent thing"* or *"A factor or influence making something necessary."*

We believe in these definitions and are happy to state that *The Significant 7 Imperatives For Delivering Successful Change In Complex IT Projects* are true urgent calls to action as illustrated in the proceeding chapters.

We have wandered through the various challenges that these pose, including: technological, skill shortages, gap between business understanding and that of IT, budget pressures, loss of control, and vested interests.

We discussed the imperative for a strategic direction and how the linkage between strategic direction, business architecture, systems architecture, and technology architecture can help improve the chances of success that your conceptual idea becomes a reality.

Various methods to breakdown complexity were explored so that there is a clear way to explain the changes ahead along with the need for them.

Then, structures in which to store the information in, to assist in retaining the linkages, were discussed with examples.

The key imperatives for delivering success were exposed showing the characteristics or attributes believed necessary, along with questions to ask in order to check if they exist in your programme and how they can apply to different initiatives.

This leads us to summarise – What are the Significant 7 Imperatives For Delivering Successful Change in Complex IT Projects? We believe they are:

1. **Lead through change** - Successful projects and IT change do not simply *just happen* by themselves. Employ effective project leadership that will coach and augment existing resources and will build and engender complete support from all stakeholders.

2. **Alignment and traceability** - Ensure that all project deliverables and success criteria for those involved are directly aligned to the business goals. There must also be traceable linkages between all effort and result. This requires a systematic approach from project leadership.

3. **Clarity** - Benefit paths from action to deliverable must be clearly defined. All roles, responsibilities, and values, relevant to all involved, must be properly identified and explicitly represented to ensure effective and efficient project governance.

4. **Consequential connection** - During projects, all action or inaction will have consequences. Operational changes, workloads, problems, or external events must be rapidly identified, and their impact immediately assessed, so that changes can be made to ensure a successful outcome. Even the best laid out plans must be able to adapt to changing circumstances.

5. **Sharp focus** - Pay careful attention to all details and strive to understand any and all interdependencies across the entire project. If delivery slips, take immediate remedial action. Ensure

full, frank and open communication throughout the entire project team so that problems do not go unnoticed or unattended.

6. **Strategic structure** - Take a strategic approach from the outset and build from an enterprise-grade foundation of business, system, and technology components. Identify and understand the differences and linkages between business processes, the capabilities required to support them, and the specific underpinning technologies.

7. **Support** - Projects must be run on a positive and assertive, not a negative or defensive, footing. If teams are overburdened, then support must be found. If specific skills are not available internally, then bring them in for the duration required to ensure the project delivers.

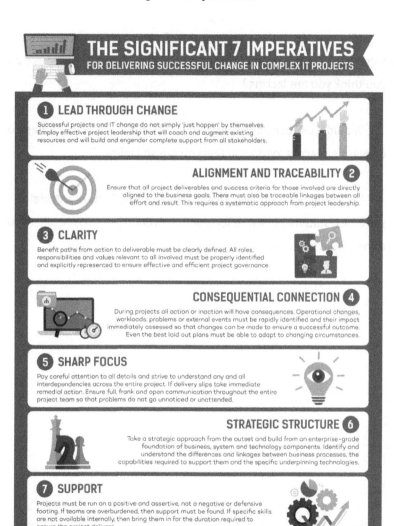

Please visit www.thedigitaltransformationbook.com to download a full colour copy of this poster.

So, where do you rank yourself, or your initiative, on the Significant 7 Imperatives? Which do you think you have and where do you think you are lacking?

Would you consider yourself a visionary when it comes to delivering success, or do you feel you are still ad-hoc?

Why not review our Significant 7 Imperatives Maturity Model and see which statement best reflects your current style, and see what you think would work best for your organisation.

Imperative	Characteristic	Maturity level 0 Minimal - Ad hoc (Unconsciously Incompetent)
Lead through change	Project leadership position	no one in place, no one noticing, no structure, no progress checking
	Senior management attitude	Not aware of what's happening, not showing any interest or involvement
	Leadership coaching	No one wants to put head above parapet, a 'manage not lead' culture
Alignment and traceability	Business goals	No one really knows the business goals, people too focused on day to day to care
	Communication between IT & business groups	plenty of emails, usually heated or defensive
	Links between business goals &project activities	Business doesn't want to own anything, IT picks up and drops whatever its interested in, people are not engaged
Clarity	Roles and responsibilities	No one really knows what they're doing, the wrong people are given responsibility
	Project cost assessment	Not known, no one worries about costs until after, try to fit the work to the allocated budget
	Benefit path	benefits not known, people only care about personal impact, not the business
Consequential connection	Dependency planning	Projects seem to fail for no reason, or be delayed by things outside our control
	Impact assessment	Cross our fingers and hope, leave it to someone else, not my problem
	Process for linking IT projects to business	Ad hoc or nothing, IT doesn't understand the business, business is too demanding
Sharp focus	Communications	Messages come 'out of the blue', no one ever tells me what's going on
	Review processes	Might be reviewed at the end, people involved have moved on
	Project structure	People brought in as a when required, if available, staff churn high
Strategic structure	Strategic/ exec level vision	Not thought about, everything is tactical, just do it and ask questions later
	Business, System & Technology	Architecture, what architecture? Lots of legacy IT that no one knows what it does
	Data sets	no one knows what we have, we have data everywhere, can never find it
Support	Workload	No one knows, constant firefighting, high staff churn
	Internal resourcing	over-stretched, no one really knows who does what, internal politics
	External partnerships	Do it all ourselves, nobody understands our business like we do

Imperative	Characteristic	Maturity level 1 **Average practice - Reactive** **(Consciously Incompetent)**
Lead through change	Project leadership position	Problem flagged up, looking for volunteers
	Senior management attitude	Struggle to get top level support
	Leadership coaching	Coaching is done by managers
Alignment and traceability	Business goals	Being investigated
	Communication between IT & business groups	Some meetings & mutual understanding more to be done
	Links between business goals &project activities	Aware of the need, looking at tools that might help
Clarity	Roles and responsibilities	Working with job titles, not project roles
	Project cost assessment	Part understood, clarification being sought on some items
	Benefit path	In process of determining business benefits
Consequential connection	Dependency planning	Pipeline of work partly understood
	Impact assessment	Aware of certain risks, but not their impact
	Process for linking IT projects to business	Aware of the need, looking at tools that might help
Sharp focus	Communications	Not enough to keep everyone up to speed
	Review processes	Project reviews only when serious problems happen
	Project structure	Ad hoc, but being formalised
Strategic structure	Strategic/ exec level vision	Being worked on
	Business, System & Technology	Work in progress to define different aspects
	Data sets	Aware of diverse or unstructured datasets
Support	Workload	Aware that it's pretty much full time firefighting
	Internal resourcing	Difficult to get the right people transferred in to projects
	External partnerships	Aware of need to reach out to build partner relationships

Imperative	Characteristic	Maturity level 2 Best practice - Proactive (Consciously Competent)
	Project leadership position	Actively recruiting for right person for the position
Lead through change	Senior management attitude	Support generally given when requested
	Leadership coaching	Already used external coaches in other functions
	Business goals	Identified
Alignment and traceability	Communication between IT & business groups	Regular meetings between senior business & IT staff
	Links between business goals &project activities	Defining most of it, generally after the event
	Roles and responsibilities	Everyone assigned roles once project underway
Clarity	Project cost assessment	Main items costed, some gaps
	Benefit path	Some implied linkages between costs and benefits
	Dependency planning	Has mapped out pipeline of work in terms of times and resources
Consequential connection	Impact assessment	Aware of risks and their immediate impact
	Process for linking IT projects to business	Documenting most of it, generally after the event
	Communications	Those who need to know are kept in the loop
Sharp focus	Review processes	Regular reviews involved selected participants in the project
	Project structure	Fully defined and committed project team in advance
	Strategic/ exec level vision	Has been defined
Strategic structure	Business, System & Technology	Done technology architecture, working on system and business
	Data sets	Rationalising datasets, building a consistent data architecture
	Workload	Mix of operational commitments and strategic projects
Support	Internal resourcing	Internal resources can be freed or made available on request
	External partnerships	Ad hoc relationships on a project by project basis

Imperative	Characteristic	Maturity level 3 Service oriented (Unconsciously Competent)
Lead through change	Project leadership position	Internal champion/leader in place
	Senior management attitude	Authority generally delegated already - trusted
	Leadership coaching	Already used leadership coaching
Alignment and traceability	Business goals	Already known and understood
	Communication between IT & business groups	IT embedded in business, regular communications at all levels
	Links between business goals &project activities	Well defined before projects started and adapted during
Clarity	Roles and responsibilities	Project team formation and roles are predetermined and understood
	Project cost assessment	Fully costed
	Benefit path	Explicit links between investment costs and benefits
Consequential connection	Dependency planning	Pipeline plus contingency plans and processes in place
	Impact assessment	Fully aware of risks and has plans in place to mitigate their impact
	Process for linking IT projects to business	Well documented before projects started and adapted during
Sharp focus	Communications	Everyone knows what's going on
	Review processes	Regular and open review involving all levels on project
	Project structure	Well defined from outset, but adaptable to allow changes
Strategic structure	Strategic/ exec level vision	In place, widely known and understood
	Business, System & Technology	All 3 separated in principal, work on definitions not complete
	Data sets	Common & consistent data architecture in place
Support	Workload	Mostly planned and able to cope with occasional emergencies
	Internal resourcing	Database of internal skills already available
	External partnerships	Some formalised partner relationships to be called upon

Digital Transformation

Imperative	Characteristic	Maturity level 4 Visionary (Incorporated as Culture)
Lead through change	Project leadership position	Clear internal leader already identified or external has been sought
	Senior management attitude	Management is fully bought in and has delegated authority
	Leadership coaching	Program of internal & external coaches in most functions
Alignment and traceability	Business goals	Already known, understood, ranked and prioritised
	Communication between IT & business groups	Already have job rotations, full engagement and understanding
	Links between business goals &project activities	There is always a comprehensive definition on all projects
Clarity	Roles and responsibilities	Establish culture of those best suited volunteering to take on roles in complex projects
	Project cost assessment	Always fully costed with contingencies, dependencies and consequences
	Benefit path	Explicit and implicit benefits are always evaluated for all major project elements
Consequential connection	Dependency planning	Complete picture of dependencies is in place before projects start
	Impact assessment	Risk impact assessment is a fundamental part of all projects
	Process for linking IT projects to business	Comprehensive documentation is provided on all projects
Sharp focus	Communications	Everyone always knows and understands what's going on
	Review processes	Ongoing review & adjustment, open feedback, no blame apportionment
	Project structure	Well defined structure, plus available pool of resources to call upon
Strategic structure	Strategic/ exec level vision	A mantra that shapes projects & organisational culture
	Business, System & Technology	All 3 are well defined and understood
	Data sets	Strong data architecture & valuable working analytics tools are already in use
Support	Workload	Fully planned from outset and has been able to cope with emergencies
	Internal resourcing	Established program of internal rotation through projects already in place
	External partnerships	Fully established & managed partner ecosystem

If you would like more information about this, or any other topic raised in the book, please visit www.thedigitaltransformation book.com to contact us.

Framework in action:

"After a period of significant growth that showed little sign of slowing, our European and central Asian client looked at their IT strategy, that has not changed since their divestment eight years previously, with a view to ensuring it was sufficient to support the business growth strategy and increasing client expectations.

Reporting to the board, we had a short time to evaluate the current IT capability, then provide and lead the implementation of a plan for the future. The role encompasses all facets with a keen entrepreneurial approach. Key considerations are in the acceleration of change, improving change success, information and cyber security, instigating an 'always on' mentality, and improving the business members experience and productivity."

ABOUT THE AUTHORS

MARTIN SHARP

As an enterprise architect and strategic thinker, Martin consistently brings technical clarity to the most complex client issues. Navigating the complex and ever-changing IT landscape, Martin's pragmatic solutions deliver change and realise business benefit within every organisation.

Martin Sharp has worked in the IT industry since 1993 and has developed an eclectic variety of skills in management and strategy, along with a breadth and depth of technical knowledge and experience. Clients have described him as knowledgeable, personable, refreshing, unbiased, and diligent – a breath of fresh air in a world where IT complexity often seems to create as many challenges as it solves.

As an enterprise architect, IT solutions & technology consultant, Martin is an enthusiastic leader, helping companies to structure their IT so that it becomes a business enabler, not a barrier to communication & growth.

His career has provided him with experience across a wide range of sectors from pharmaceuticals, aerospace companies, universities, councils, motor and drinks manufacturers, airport operators, hospitals, through to smaller local businesses. Martin has advised thousands of company IT users and improved the way they interact with their IT devices and consumer IT services. These include companies such as HSBC, ITV, Kinstellar, Spire Healthcare, Circle Healthcare, Heathrow Airport, PAREXEL International, GlaxoSmithKline, Novartis, Manchester Airport Group, Gatwick Airport, University College London, Close Brothers, Global Collect, ING Bank, Ioko, Affini Technology, Platform Consultancy, CommCare, Platform-Smart and Bliss-Systems.

When not working, he enjoys spending time with his family, exploring, learning, having fun, and simply being together.

Currently, Martin owns and operates multiple ventures within the IT consultancy, business consultancy, coaching, and mentoring arena. He also invests his time, money, and resources in helping aspiring entrepreneurs and investors fulfil their potential.

EDWARD JOHNS

With an excellent pedigree in structuring, mobilising, recovering and delivering enterprise IT change initiatives, Edward's track record of IT change in high availability, time constrained initiatives, is unparalleled. Bringing to bear strong methodology and process balance, Edward focuses on change to deliver maximum business benefit to our clients.

Ed has a strong record of achievement in delivering leading edge technology transformation, strategic definition, enterprise programme delivery, and business change initiatives through leadership of structured programme teams.

His programme management and director level delivery capability is underpinned by a broad experience base that spans a wide range of industry sectors, geographic locations, and cultural dimensions from overall programme ownership to project mobilisation, rationalisation, service transition, targeted benefits realisation, and failure recovery.

These include working with VISA, PAREXEL International, Heathrow Airport, Manchester Airport Group, KPMG Europe, Jardine Lloyd Thompson, Barclays Capital, KPMG International, DHL Systems, Allianz Cornhill and Affini Technology.

Primarily reporting to CIO level, he has built a solid reputation for delivering business, technology, service and operational transformations that have enabled significant cost, productivity, reputational and operational benefit realisation.

With this book, Edward and Martin have shared a combined 45 years of experience and in depth analysis that have helped many businesses across the world increase their bottom line profits, decrease their overall costs, and take on the challenges of tomorrow by keeping their IT transformation programmes under control.

IMPERATORS

Imperators – delivering successful change in complex IT projects

Imperators is a collective of experienced IT leadership and business change specialists. It has seen many organisations become embroiled in tricky situations with failing projects and stumbling change initiatives. Rather than simply providing extra manpower or effort, Imperators offers a step change in project direction and leadership through its unique synthesis of industry best practices and leading methodologies.

Imperators was born with the ideology of helping its clients straight though the problem and directing them to the heart of the solution. The name *Imperators* sums up the ideology and vision; this is not about being passengers on your journey, but a purposeful driving force to your desired business outcome.

The team at Imperators has built a network of excellence that has taken 20 years to construct. This provides a wealth of experience and specialism direct to any project or initiative reducing overhead and avoiding delays. Deep client relationships, with sustainable levels of support and expert advice, deliver long-term benefits for Imperators' customers.

Imperators delivers on the imperatives for IT project success:

- Rapid engagement, decisive action, project leadership
- Board and executive level engagement bridging business and IT
- Synthesis of industry best practices and leading methodologies
- Strategic and structured project leadership
- Focus, purpose, direction
- Results that clearly meet business needs

Drive Change,

Deliver Results,

Depend on Imperators

Email: info@imperators.com

Web: www.imperators.com

Twitter: @theimperators

WHERE DID THE NAME IMPERATORS COME FROM?

When the Emperors of Rome had a problem or needed something resolved, often, the only way to ensure a successful outcome, was to go and resolve it themselves. At the later stages of the Roman Empire, for an Emperor to leave Rome and direct his legions on the ground, was a high risk strategy, so, the Imperator was born. The Imperator was a trusted agent of the Emperor who was given the resources needed to action the Emperors will and resolve the issue at hand.

They were chosen from the highest ranks of the Roman armies and selected for being resourceful, direct, pragmatic, and sometimes brutal, in fulfilling the task or achieving the outcome. The Imperator had the advantage of being able to look at the problem from a fresh perspective and bring resources to bear rapidly and directly.

We, at Imperators, like to think this analogy demonstrates our core ethos and ideology. We are able to bring our experience to the heart of your challenge and direct you and your resources rapidly toward a successful outcome. That's the value add we bring to the table – that's the imperator's way.

We are not here to be passengers on your journey, we are here to help you lead it.

Drive Change,

Deliver Results,

Depend on Imperators